Autism and Diet

of related interest

The AiA Gluten and Dairy Free Cookbook
Foreword by Rosemary Kessick, Allergy Induced Autism
Compiled by Marilyn Le Breton
ISBN 978 1 84310 067 6

A User Guide to the GF/CF Diet for Autism, Asperger Syndrome and AD/HD
Luke Jackson
Foreword by Marilyn Le Breton
ISBN 978 1 84310 055 3

Diet Intervention and Autism
Implementing the Gluten Free and Casein Free Diet for Autistic Children and Adults – A Practical Guide for Parents
Marilyn Le Breton
Foreword by Rosemary Kessick, Allergy Induced Autism
ISBN 978 1 85302 935 6

Autism, Brain, and Environment
Richard Lathe
ISBN 978 1 84310 438 4

Autism and Diet

What You Need to Know

Rosemary Kessick

Jessica Kingsley Publishers
London and Philadelphia

First published in 2009
by Jessica Kingsley Publishers
116 Pentonville Road
London N1 9JB, UK
and
400 Market Street, Suite 400
Philadelphia, PA 19106, USA

www.jkp.com

No information in this book is to be construed as medical advice and neither the author nor the publishers take any responsibility for any decision taken by the reader as a result of this information. Always consult a qualified medical practitioner before implementing dietary intervention and where any medical condition is suspected.

Library of Congress Cataloging in Publication Data
Kessick, Rosemary.
    Autism and diet : what you need to know / Rosemary Kessick.
        p. cm.
    Includes bibliographical references and index.
    ISBN 978-1-84310-983-9 (pb : alk. paper)   1. Autism--Nutritional aspects. 2. Autism--Diet therapy. I. Title.
    RC553.A88K47 2009
    616.85'882--dc22

                                                    2008042026

British Library Cataloguing in Publication Data
A CIP catalogue record for this book is available from the British Library

ISBN 978 1 84310 983 9

Printed and bound in the United States by
Thomson-Shore, 7300 Joy Road, Dexter, MI 48130

To all those who have been
concerned enough to observe,
intelligent enough to hypothesize,
motivated enough to test and
brave enough to stick by their
findings…

…true scientists with open minds
and caring hearts.

Thank you.

Contents

Introduction

Connections between the symptoms of autism and the foods we eat have been observed for decades but for many years the science behind the connection was evasive. Many of us have worked with dietary and environmental interventions for years and today we see a growing body of scientific research available to back up parental and professional observations. This research shows that a subgroup of autistic children and adults are adversely affected by certain foods and non-foods which can harm the developing brain and cause autistic behaviours.

More expertise in the use of dietary intervention in autism spectrum disorder has brought with it a wealth of excellent publications on the subject and sessions are frequently given over to discussion of same at conferences worldwide. The internet, meanwhile, affords instant access to huge swathes of information on the subject.

Unfortunately, however well-versed a parent or primary carer might be through diligent study, attending conferences and so on, passing the knowledge on to the wider audience of people concerned in the care and treatment of their children still remains a difficulty.

Time and money are all at a premium and parents have persistently asked for a pocket guide of basic information to give to befuddled family, friends, teachers, therapists and nurses, providing a bite-sized explanation for those who can't face the whole plateful!

After reading *Autism and Diet – What You Need to Know*, you may be sure that you will be armed with basic tools to help you implement dietary intervention in autism safely and successfully and will be confident as to why it is necessary.

1

What is the Autistic Spectrum?

It's important to understand that autism itself is not a condition. It is a description, a general term characterized by the 'triad of impairment', a phrase originally coined by UK psychiatrist Dr Lorna Wing, to describe and categorize the behaviours of those individuals who are on what is described as a 'spectrum' or 'continuum'.

The three elements of the triad describe impairments in:

- social relationships

- communication

- imaginative thought.

The array within each of the categories can be bewildering. An impairment in social relationships can show up as an almost complete indifference to other people, a willingness to respond to interactions (though not to initiate them) or a willingness to initiate interactions with others that is displayed in an odd, inappropriate or repetitive way.

Communication deficits may be manifest in a number of ways. There may be a total lack of speech, with poor understanding of verbal and non-verbal communication. There is sometimes repetitive or echolalic speech (literally echoing what someone else says), or even well-developed speech, seemingly irrelevant to the given social context demonstrating a general lack of understanding of what others are talking about.

Deficits in imaginative thought range from the inability to invent an imaginary world or to copy and use pretend play, through to the unimaginative use of toys or use of any objects inappropriately or for sensation only.

Early signs, like lining objects up or colour-coding blocks and toys are often noted, whilst interests may be rigid and stereotyped. Repetitive behaviours can feature, from a topic of extra-special interest, which seems all-consuming, through to repetitive body movements or routines which must be adhered to.

It's very easy to get confused about the causes of autism when it seems as if every week brings a fresh news story about the 'cause', genetic or otherwise. It is also often reported that there is 'no known cause of autism' but this isn't strictly true as in many cases of autism spectrum disorder (ASD) the cause of the autistic symptoms may be attributed to a metabolic condition, viral or bacterial infection or genetic basis. Head injury has also been identified with autism.

From the management point of view, it's more appropriate for this primer to focus on the symptoms rather than the cause. It's worth knowing, though, that in 2001, faced with a sharp increase in autism, the UK Medical Research Council (MRC) held a review into the causes. Medical experts involved in the review agreed that the origin of the condition was understood in an estimated 4 per cent of cases.

A host of disorders make up this 4 per cent, but to those who remain aghast at the idea that diet may in any way, shape or form have anything to do with cause, effect or control of autistic symptoms, two conditions might be of particular interest.

One is phenylketonuria, commonly known as 'PKU'. This is an inherited metabolic defect in protein metabolism. Because of a defective gene, the liver is unable to convert phenylalanine to tyrosine, resulting in a build-up of phenylalanine in the blood, which eventually passes into the brain, causing mental retardation and other neurological problems, including autism. This condition is controlled by limiting protein-containing foods which, as well as the obvious sources like meat, eggs, dairy and nuts, also include most wheat products, such as pasta and bread, and some fruit, like oranges and cherries.

A second well-documented cause of autism is purine autism, where the body excretes too much uric acid. Gout is in the same constellation of purine disorders where dietary intervention is used to control the symptoms.

The main dietary intervention in autism which we will discuss in this guide is based on scientific studies from around the world. Initial observations were made at the University of Florida in the early 1970s and the greater part of the scientific work was carried out in Norway by neuropaediatrician Professor Karl Reichelt.

As medical history demonstrates, observation of patients by their doctors and those closest to them is the starting point for research which can lead to both an effective treatment of the symptoms and an understanding of the causes and natures of the condition. Anyone with whom the autistic child or adult spends a great deal of time can provide unique input and vital insights to this process of understanding.

2

The History of Dietary Intervention in Autism

The gluten-free/casein-free (GF/CF) diet

Early observations were made by Dr Jak Panksepp in the USA. He identified abnormal substances in the urine of autistic children, which turned out to be derived from food-stuffs. The story was taken up by Dr Karl Reichelt at the University of Oslo; he had a particular interest in the schizophrenias but soon recognized that the findings applied to a section of the autistic population.

Delving deeper, he identified the two abnormalities as coming from foods normally in our diets: dairy produce, wheat, oats, barley, spelt and rye.

The abnormal compounds Dr Reichelt was by now consistently finding in urine samples turned out to be in the same family as heroin and, he hypothesized, as many of the physical symptoms he was finding were almost identical to those displayed in cases of heroin or morphine use and misuse, if those foods were removed from the diet then the symptoms should get better.

Reichelt tested the hypothesis and found that removing the offending foods resulted in a startling improvement in a whole array of symptoms, both behavioural and physical.

Parents were reporting huge improvements in their children, ranging from better behaviour to improvement in the ability to concentrate and learn. At this stage the observations had not been formalized until a double-blind study was carried out in conjunction with educationalist Dr Ann-Mari Knivsberg.

This study was robust enough to satisfy the scientific world, showing conclusively that in a subset of the autistic population, removal of gluten and casein from the diet is of enormous benefit.

Sulphates and salicylates

Several years later, in the UK, toxicologist Dr Rosemary Waring from Birmingham University carried out different tests; these were on blood samples from autistic children. Her aim was to identify how efficiently their bodies were carrying out a different biochemical reaction. Primarily interested in how certain foods were affecting migraine sufferers, Dr Waring noted that these children, in line with allergy sufferers, were deficient in their ability to detoxify a number of compounds from their bodies, compounds found in many everyday foods and household compounds.

Dietary intervention was to prove trickier here and not as clear-cut as the gluten and casein story, because Dr Waring's observations were that individual autistic children had a limited and differing ability to clear the system of waste compounds. In addition, the Birmingham findings tied in with a number of other previous observations on the biological functioning or, rather, non-functioning, of many autistic children. The plot was thickening!

The inefficiency to detoxify the body must be taken into consideration alongside other dietary approaches.

The specific carbohydrate diet

Researchers and clinicians have been interested in the connection between diet and mental symptoms for many years. At the beginning of the twentieth century, doctors working with coeliac patients who also suffered from schizophrenic-type symptoms observed degeneration of nervous tissue, spinal cord and the brain, which they attributed to malabsorption of vital vitamins and minerals. Heated scientific discussions took place in the 1950s between scientists who argued, on one hand, that gluten, the protein found in wheat, rye, barley and spelt, was the cause of coeliac disease whilst, on the other, others postulated that it was the carbohydrate component causing the mischief.

This early work was carried out by Dr Sidney Haas and later with his son Dr Merrill Hass, who together pioneered a diet called the 'specific carbohydrate diet' (SCD) which limits the type of carbohydrate intake to monosaccharides. This diet has proved successful in controlling Crohn's disease, ulcerative colitis and gluten-free diet-resistant coeliac disease because altering the nutritional intake controls overgrowth and imbalance of intestinal microbial flora. Recently, many children on the autistic spectrum suffering with gastrointestinal disease have also shown dramatic improvements on the SCD diet.

The ketogenic diet

Another diet which has been used when there is intractable epilepsy is the 'ketogenic diet', which is a high fat, very low carbohydrate, adequate protein mix. This diet can be successful but must be implemented under strict medical supervision.

Liquid feeds

Finally, though not within the scope of this publication, children and adults who suffer from serious inflammatory bowel disease may be prescribed a liquid feed by their doctor. This doesn't refer to liquidized food: these feeds are specially formulated products available on prescription which provide total nutrition required for body and brain growth in a form allowing efficient absorption by the diseased gastrointestinal tract and easy assimilation by the body.

Today, many children and adults with autism have benefited from dietary intervention of all sorts. The benefits range from complete eradication of autistic symptoms and gastrointestinal symptoms to regulated sleep patterns and the ability to learn more effectively.

Care must always be taken to follow some basic steps when instigating and continuing with dietary or environmental intervention for the autistic spectrum disorders. The rewards can be great but the pitfalls are many.

The low oxalate diet

Very recently, interest has been aroused in the role of oxalates in autism. Researchers have found low levels of glutathione in autistic patients who have sulphation pathway issues. Following the biochemical trail, combined with observations of which foods seem to be causing symptoms, including pain, has led to some parents trying a low oxalate diet. Although this seems to be promising in some cases, caution is necessary and the diet should be tried in collaboration with a dietician, and only after ongoing dietary analysis suggests that high oxalate foods may be causing problems.

3

A Whistle-stop Guide to the Science Behind the Interventions

Opioid excess

Neurochemist and medical doctor Karl Reichelt found abnormal peptides in the urine of people with autism. Now, *very simply*, peptides are the family of short molecules formed from the linking, in a defined order, of various amino acids and are used as the building blocks of proteins.

The majority of the peptides Reichelt found are derived from dietary gluten or casein, or both.

Gluten is a protein found in wheat, rye, barley, oats and spelt, while casein is the protein found in *all* animal milks and the products made from them.

So, basically, the peptides found in the urine of the autistic children are unbroken-down forms of proteins from milk and certain cereal products.

And here's the interesting and crucial bit.

The unbroken-down bits, called 'beta-casomorphin' and 'gluteomorphin' or 'gliadinomorphin', are opioid-like substances. Think morphine or heroin and you'll get the basic drift.

If you look down a list of symptoms of a heroin addict, it reads eerily like a list of symptoms for the children who fall into this category. Opioids:

- suppress pain sensation
- cause constipation
- constrict pupils
- cause hallucinations
- cause slow gait
- impair night vision
- slow respiration
- cause itchiness
- prevent feelings of pain, fear, hunger and cold.

So, these peptides are biologically active, meaning that they do things to the system, and importantly, the functioning of the brain. This is why, when you take away the foods that are producing the peptides, the symptoms disappear.

Children and adults whose urine indicates high levels of urinary peptides from gluten and casein will only benefit if every trace of casein and gluten is removed from their diet and environment and no contamination whatsoever occurs.

The question is: how did the peptides get into the system from the gut? This leads us on to sulphation.

Sulphation

There are two major detoxification systems in the body, one of which is the sulphation system, by means of an enzyme group called 'phenol sulphur transferase' (PST). Dr Rosemary Waring, a toxicologist from Birmingham University, discovered that autistic children and adults have significantly impaired ability to detox their systems owing to a deficit of PST. Some have a very low capacity to oxidize sulphur compounds, a problem strongly associated with chemical and food allergies, whilst others have a low sulphotransferase level and are unable to fully metabolize phenols and amines and some have both problems.

Now this detox system is important in the story because PST not only detoxes internal systems like used neurotransmitters such as serotonin, dopamine and noradrenaline, but also external toxins, phenolic compounds and salicylates commonly found in highly coloured natural foods as well as many cleaning products.

So, with a deficit in PST, the child is storing up used toxins in the body and circulating them.

Additionally, many commonly used drugs, such as paracetamol, use this pathway to break down and clear themselves out of the body, so if there is a fault then more toxins are stored in the body and circulated. Normal breakdown on this pathway is also involved in numerous other mechanisms in the body, such as gastric hormone formation, the methionine pathways and essential breakdown of other compounds.

Finally, the sulphation system is vital in maintaining the mucous membranes of the body and the matrix which makes up the integrity of the gut. So, if there's a problem with sulphation then the division between the brain and the blood, known as the 'blood–brain barrier', is impaired. The gut will be 'leaky', letting toxins out of the gut into the bloodstream and through to the brain.

Not only do the opioids slip through the net, but so do nasty toxins that are contained in compacted faeces. Compacted faeces become lodged in the gut because of constipation, itself caused by, among other things, opioids.

The sulphation system difficulty isn't as easy to control as opioid excess because each individual is impaired to a greater or lesser degree, resulting in their having a different level of tolerance, and it would be virtually impossible to strip all phenols and salicylates from the diet and environment. The best thing we can do is to reduce the load to a level where the individual can cope. This means cleaning up the environment as much as possible and not exposing the susceptible individual to obviously toxic products.

Carbohydrate digestion and the specific carbohydrate diet

Carbohydrate is the body's basic dietary fuel and it takes one of three different forms. Primarily there are the simple sugars called 'monosaccharides', which are glucose, fructose and galactose. These sugars when ingested are absorbed directly into the bloodstream through the intestinal lining.

If too much simple sugar is eaten at one go it can result in a 'sugar high'. The pancreas responds to the influx of simple sugar by releasing insulin to prevent blood glucose levels from rising too high, and in consequence the blood sugar levels drop rapidly after around three hours. The counter-response in the body is a surging release of adrenaline, which can cause irritability.

The second type of carbohydrate is the 'disaccharide' or 'double sugar'. There are four types of disaccharide: lactose, sucrose, maltose and isomaltose, all requiring enzymes (catalysts for specific reactions) to split them down in order to allow the body to digest them. The breakdown of the disaccharides occurs in the microvilli on the borders of the villi, frond-like projections which, together with folds in the submucosa, significantly increase the absorptive surface of the small intestine. The enzymes are incorporated in the membranes of the microvilli.

The last type of carbohydrates are the complex carbohydrates, 'polysaccharides' or plant starches made up of chains of glucose molecules which, like the disaccharides, the body cannot digest before breaking right down into component molecules. There are two sorts of starch, 'amylase' and 'amylopectin', which are found in varying proportions in different plants.

Normally, the large bowel is the major site of bacterial colonization where gut bacteria and starch interact and ferment. Efficient gastric secretions and rapid peristalsis in the well-functioning body tend to limit numbers of bacteria in the small bowel. The digestive system of many autistic children and adults, on the other hand, is far from normal.

'Hypochlorhydria', underproduction of stomach acid, together with intestinal motor dysfunction resulting in severely compromised peristalsis, both cause substantial 'bad' bacterial overgrowth of the small bowel, which can result in ongoing mucosal injury. The basis of the specific carbohydrate diet (SCD) is to deprive the bacteria of food thus preventing fermentation, bloating, increase of organic acids, inhibition of enzyme production in the microvilli and other associated abnormalities.

The SCD provides the body with only those carbohydrates that require the minimum of digestion so the body benefits from them rather than the bad bacteria benefiting. Once the bacteria die off, the villi and microvilli begin to produce enzymes again so that nutrients may be absorbed efficiently. The goblet cells, which have been overproducing mucous, normalize and the immune system, nourished once more, begins to fight back. The SCD is, as its name suggests, very specific and should be undertaken only under the strict guidance of an experienced dietician overseen by a gastroenterologist. That said, in cases where other dietary measures have shown limited success and symptoms and gastrointestinal symptoms are still severe, it is worth considering. Owing to the very specialist nature of the diet the foods are not included in this publication, but the reader is referred to the Bibliography at the end of the book.

Back to Basics

We hear that a great number of people are put off dietary intervention because they don't understand it, don't know why they should be doing it, have no family support, no medical support, think it's going to be too expensive or are just too confused by all the information out there. Equally, we often hear of people who thought that they were following dietary intervention with their child, didn't see any results and gave up.

When to consider a special diet

Those most likely to benefit from the intervention are those who, when they start sliding into autism, modify their own diet and become picky eaters. They limit the foods they eat and consume them to excess. The foods they crave are the very foods causing the mischief and their menu often reads: milk, bread, pasta, chicken nuggets, squash and yoghurts. This is usually in sharp contrast to the normal diet they enjoyed from birth as this category tends to be a regressive form of autism. In addition, these children may also display physical problems like low muscle tone. Some children are obviously hooked on highly coloured sweets or snack foods like flavoured crisps whilst others have marked gastrointestinal symptoms.

Getting started

Once you've identified that dietary intervention is appropriate, you need to work out a plan of action and understand what to expect. These days there's a great deal of information on the internet about diet and biomedical interventions and it can be very confusing working out where to start, what to buy and how to proceed. From now on this book is written from the stance of the gluten/casein/additive-free diet, although the reviews and checklists apply equally to other diets.

The key is to *keep it simple*.

- Begin by filling in the checklist of common classic symptoms from the Resources. This will give you an idea where the main problems lie and you can go back to it and review it after a couple of months.

- Fill in a daily diet sheet (see the Resources) for a full week. This will achieve two things. It will serve as a baseline for nutrient analysis and show you, and the wider team involved, what the quality of the original diet was at the start. A frequent criticism from friends, family and, sadly, professionals, is that the new exclusion diet will deprive the child or adult of nutrients and of things they like. A record of intake to refer back to is invaluable as, more often than not, it shows how inadequate the original diet was.

- Contact the doctor. Explain what you are going to embark on and ask for help in the form of a referral to a *qualified dietician*. This is where the diet diary comes in useful because it may now be analysed to identify the exact make-up of the intake with a full breakdown of vitamins, minerals, proteins, carbohydrates and fats. If your doctor is loath to make a referral or there isn't a dietician available, it's worth paying for a private appointment. The second important thing to do *before* taking gluten out of the diet is to ask the doctor to carry out a blood test for coeliac disease.

• Know your ingredients. Read round the subject and start to read labels. Remember that many, if not most, processed foods contain some ingredients which don't need to be declared so you have to be absolutely sure that the product is sound. If this is too daunting for you then you may decide to cook everything from scratch; this way you have full control and can avoid slip-ups.

• Remember that you are dealing with the sort of cravings a heroin addict would have. Take an addict off their drug of choice and they go into a period of withdrawal with intense cravings and a need to find their 'fix' at all costs. The withdrawal from offending foods can take many forms: sleeplessness, rashes, screaming, self-harm, aggression or clinginess and tends to be more intense in an adult or older child. If at any stage during withdrawal you are worried then take your child to a doctor to put your mind at rest. Be prepared for withdrawal and remember that whilst some get away with minimal withdrawal if there is no reaction at all then you may not have cleaned the diet up completely.

- Don't forget that gluten and casein are often found in non-foods. Screen your washing up liquids, shampoos, soaps and clothes washing powder or liquid. Telephone the manufacturers to be sure.

- Remember that it can take up to a year to get rid of traces of gluten from the system, while casein disappears within a few weeks.

- If you decide to take the casein out first and then follow on by removing the gluten then that's fine, but both must come out.

- Take aspartame, monosodium glutamate and monopotassium glutamate out right away. They are poisoning your child and will cancel out the benefits of taking out the gluten and casein.

- Take all artificial colourings, preservatives and flavourings (natural or artificial) out straight away.

- Take nitrites and nitrates out straight away.

- See the list in the Resources but remember that gluten is found in wheat, oats, barley, rye and spelt whilst casein is found in *all* animal milks, including human breast milk, though in much smaller concentrations than other animals.

- Don't worry if at first your child turns his or her nose up at what you are offering. They can *smell* out the gluten and casein and if it's not on the plate then they may not be interested. Unless they have seriously advanced gut disease which is making eating and drinking very painful they will eat something, even if it's a week on chips. (But watch the salt, which may have an anti-caking agent in it to help it flow; if you must use salt use pure sea salt.)

- If you are going to try this or any other diet for that matter, then remember that it must be followed 100 per cent or it's a waste of everyone's time.

Methods of approach

That sounds a bit like describing an aircraft coming in to land! That being the case, you probably want as easy a touchdown as possible so here are the alternatives.

- Rip everything out of your cupboards and restock them or leave them bare for the time being. Stock up with absolutely basic unprocessed safe foods, including something safe you know your child will like, batten down the hatches and prepare for withdrawal. The advantages of this method are that you can get withdrawal and cravings over in the minimum of time and may start to see improvements quite quickly. On the other hand, the intensity of withdrawal may be frightening for both your child and you or the rest of the family. Beginning the diet this way with autism spectrum disorder (ASD) adults can be very challenging.

- The other way is to remove the casein-containing products first over a few weeks followed by the gluten. (Casein is easier to spot for the beginner.) Then follow by taking out the products that are problematic for the phenol sulphur transferase (PST) -deficient. Whichever method you choose, a 'cook everything from scratch in the first place' approach will ensure that you reach the best baseline from which to move forwards. Supermarket food is a nightmare: even frozen vegetables can be glazed with casein, some chicken breast has a casein mix injected into it and rice mixes can have gluten in them.

- If you have good reason to suspect that the sulphation system is deficient, for example if you see a lot of red ear reactions and dark circles under the eyes, then sulphation issues might be part of the picture. If this is the case then you can remove the main offenders at the start of the diet as well. Sulphation is responsible for clearing amines, phenols, salicylates (a type of phenol), and used neurotransmitters from the system, among other things, as well as ensuring the integrity of the blood–brain barrier and the gut. In addition, the system is used in the body to break down certain drugs like paracetamol.

It simply isn't possible to cut phenols and amines out of the picture completely but what we can do is lighten the load on the system. Using personal care products with fewer and less harsh ingredients in them and avoiding the foods known to be highest in amines, salicylates and phenols will prevent overload and allow for a little reserve such as an anaesthetic.

The foods which cause the most trouble are bananas, raspberries, citrus fruit, apples and chocolate (even the gluten- and casein-free variety; it's the chocolate itself causing the difficulty). Marmite® is also a problem and many autistic children and adults are hooked on it. Other salicylate-containing foods are cucumbers, nectarines, peaches, berries, plums, tea and tomatoes. Since many plants have a higher concentration of salicylates in the skin it's always worth trying them peeled before removing them altogether.

Many parents overlook the sulphation aspect and give up on dietary intervention too soon when they don't see an immediate improvement. Don't. If you are going to do this then you must be committed.

A clean up in the clean-up department is a must as well. Convert to simple cleaning product formulas or read up on old-fashioned ways of cleaning, which may also save you money. Investing in a steam cleaner is always a good idea too and microfibre cloths are a godsend.

Personal care products around the house are full of chemicals; if you don't believe it take a look at the list on the deodorant canister! Everything that is sprayed and squirted in the modern home has to be questioned, as has everything that touches the skin. Cut down on everything you can and change to more natural products for the whole family. Don't be fooled by the words *natural* and *organic*, though; many of these products still contain ingredients like sodium laureth sulphate and benzoates so read the labels and *keep it simple!*

Finally re-introduce your family to good old-fashioned *water*, preferably filtered through a good quality system, but if you can't afford it don't make it an excuse to keep using squash and fizzy drinks. Cut them out, now!

So, to recap, basic off-limit ingredient list for the gluten-free, casein-free and PST-deficient:

Wheat	Grapes
Oats	Bananas
Barley	Apples
Rye	Raspberries
Casein	Oranges
Monosodium glutamate	Lemons
Aspartame	Limes
Glutamates	Mandarins
Flavourings	Grapefruit
Colourings	Satsumas
Preservatives	Tomatoes
	Chocolate

Is that all?

Well no, actually; the full list, including the substances that are derived from the main offenders commonly used in food manufacture is shown in the Resources, but it's a little scary so look later on.

What next?

Typically, as the diet progresses other foods that have been causing problems come to light. You will identify these by filling in the food/behaviour diary. Remember that a reaction can be immediate or it can occur within a few hours or even days. Using the diary gives you a 'helicopter view' over a period of time enabling you to spot the source of the problem.

It's sensible to put in some basic vitamins and minerals at the beginning but it's really important to remember that they can cause problems as well so don't take out foods and put in vitamins simultaneously otherwise the picture may become very confusing.

You may want to put the vitamins and minerals in *before* you start on dietary intervention, which is fine, but be sure to add these one at a time leaving at least three weeks between the introduction of each one and a further three weeks before you start on the diet. Make absolutely sure that the ones you buy are both safe for the diet as well as of decent quality.

So why should you consider supplements?

Compromised absorption
Quite simply, those in this subgroup are not absorbing nutrients efficiently from their guts. Just how well or not in each individual case is difficult to pin down so caution is always advised.

Self-limiting diet
The ASD child or adult who limits their food for whatever reason, whether it's because they are narrowing their intake to foods that are giving them a hit, frightened of eating because of inflammation in the gut or for any other reason is, without a shadow of a doubt, lacking in essential nutrients.

Modern food production
Mass production techniques over the past 30 years or so have led to a change in the balance of nutrients in the food we eat.

Basic foods are broken up and reconstituted before being repackaged to look wholesome. Non-organic meat is pumped full of antibiotics and animals are fed on unnatural feed, while food scientists have developed ways to lengthen shelf life far beyond what is natural.

Bear in mind that the effective physiological functioning of every cell in the body, including brain cells, depends on the presence of a range of nutrients. A deficiency of one or more of these may affect a cell's ability to absorb or make use of other nutrients so it is not always possible to identify the precise effect of individual micro-nutrients. This being the case, there are some basic measures you can take to begin with.

What supplements to buy

Any vitamin or mineral has the potential to cause an adverse reaction so proceed with caution and introduce one at a time.

MAGNESIUM SULPHATE

Unfortunately there is no way of replacing sulphate except by using magnesium sulphate (Epsom salts) in the bath. This is a laxative and with many of the children already suffering from diarrhoea and an inflammatory bowel condition, oral ingestion of the bath water should be avoided. Use it sparingly to begin with, especially if you are using it with an adult, as it can kickstart the system and has been known to cause some frightening and unwanted reactions like rapid heart beat and vision disturbance.

TRACE MINERALS

Many ASD children and adults suffer from 'pica', eating non-foods. This is shared with people who suffer from inflammatory bowel disorders and rather than being a behavioural problem, denotes a deficiency. When pica is present liquid trace minerals (for easy absorption) can minimize or eradicate the problem.

CALCIUM OR MAGNESIUM MIX

Studies on coeliac children before and after removal of gluten have shown big differences in bone density even though their diet before the removal of gluten contained adequate calcium. There is plenty of calcium in foods other than dairy products but a calcium supplement together with magnesium is a wise move.

ESSENTIAL FATTY ACIDS

Take care with this one. There is an optimum balance of omega 3–6–9; generally, there is considered to be too much omega 6 in the Western diet, but as the ASD diet is disordered anyway it's hard to tell without a full analysis. A good quality mercury-free/flavouring-free/whole-body fish oil is good but some people react badly to the fish, or to some types of fish. Alternatively, a plant oil like hemp is good but some people have difficulty breaking down plant-based oils so it's a case of trial and error.

A GOOD ANTI-OXIDANT

An anti-oxidant is a must and basic selenium is excellent to start with.

A BROAD-SPECTRUM MIX

A good all-round mix of vitamins and minerals from a reputable company.

ZINC

Zinc is needed for more than 200 different enzymes in the brain and body, including those involved in cell division and replication, immune system function and the building of polyunsaturated fatty acids from the essential fatty acid pre-cursors available from vegetable sources.

In the UK it is possible to obtain vitamins and minerals on prescription so do ask your doctor. Make sure to ask for an unflavoured powder mix specifically for highly sensitive and allergic children.

Taking stock

When you think you have stabilized, are seeing improvements in behaviour, understanding, speech or bowel movements or both and want to begin to vary the diet then proceed – but with caution. You may want to re-introduce foods that don't contain gluten or dairy but which may have caused problems before to see if they can be tolerated now.

Continue to fill in a diet/behaviour sheet and only ever trial one food at a time, a small amount at first, observing and analysing all the way. Don't forget that the reaction may not be immediate so whatever you do don't be impatient.

Very rarely, gluten and casein have been re-introduced successfully after a long recovery time. Don't be fooled if your child ingests one of these two by mistake and you don't see a reaction. If you do want to try to re-introduce these then proceed with *absolute caution*.

Why might we not see any improvement?

1. You might still have a source of casein and gluten in the diet.

2. There is something seriously awry on the sulphation pathway.

3. There is an underlying gastrointestinal problem.

4. The child or adult is not in this subgroup.

5

The Offending Food Pyramid

The pyramid (Figure 5.1) is a simplified schematic in four parts to illustrate how to start and proceed through dietary intervention.

Beginning at the base of the pyramid, the first section underpinning the structure demonstrates that all foods and environmental agents containing gluten and casein must be removed. This is an absolute. If one is causing a problem so is the other, even if casomorphin hasn't shown up in the urine on an high performance liquid chromatography (HPLC) laboratory test.

Remember that every single trace must come out.

In the second section we see that monosodium glutamate, aspartame and synthetic E-numbers have to come out for everyone embarking on the diet. Although this constitutes stage two it might be noted that this section, by and large, contains the problem substances identified by Dr Ben Feingold with his work with attention deficit hyperactivity disorder (ADHD) children. There are very good reasons why *all* children should be protected permanently from these additives.

The third section concerns phenols and salicylates, as previously described. This is where the diet begins to vary from

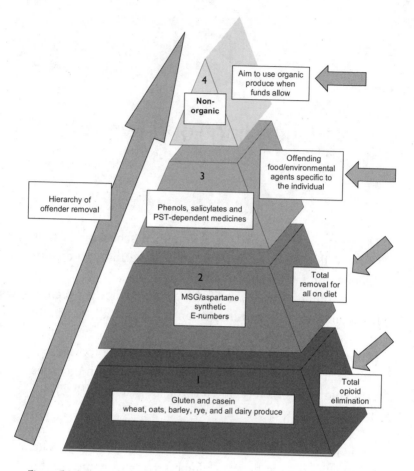

Figure 5.1 The offending food pyramid.

individual to individual. What is a major offender for one individual may be well tolerated by another, but the aim is to pinpoint problem foods and substances while adopting general good practice in the use of less harsh personal and cleaning products. Remember, 'eco-friendly' and 'organic' doesn't mean that you can be off your guard. Be vigilant at all times!

The final section refers specifically to organic food. The beauty of organic produce is that there are strict guidelines as to how it can be grown and what fertilizers and pesticides may be used, together with how much, during the growing season. Organically raised animals have had the minimum of medicines and there is growing concern about the amounts of antibiotics and growth hormones pumped routinely into non-organic animals. Labelling meat as 'natural' isn't necessarily safe as it can still contain artificial ingredients added after slaughter. Similarly, 'free-range' doesn't mean that an animal has ever been outside.

Organic food is universally more expensive than non-organic food and few hard-pressed households can afford to buy it routinely. Anything is better than nothing though. You might be able to grow your own fruit and vegetables or contact a local growers' association to help. Some organic meat is better than nothing and fish, wild not farmed, on a regular basis is good.

In a recent report, the following fruit and vegetables were deemed to be the safest to buy:

Broccoli	Pineapple
Cabbage	Avocado
Banana	Onion
Kiwi	Frozen sweet corn
Asparagus	Frozen small (sweet) peas
Mango	Aubergine

School Essentials

Educate your school

It's important for everyone to understand that these dietary and environmental measures are necessary, scientifically sound and that it's not just a fad on someone's part, be it parent, carer or child. Once you understand the nature of the condition and the preventative steps necessary to ensure the ongoing health and safety of the affected child or adult, it's *vital* that you communicate the details to everyone who is likely to come into contact with him or her.

There is a possibility that the concept will be met with disbelief. In our world of high speed, hi-tech communication we're bombarded with information, some good and some bad. Recently, allergy in general has received a great deal of attention, partly because of the huge rise in cases. Unfortunately though, we're becoming 'allergied out'! We're now so familiar with the language of food, environment, allergy and intolerance that there is a very real danger of becoming immune to the details of allergy and intolerance and dismissive of the dangers.

You need to embark on a plan of attack to educate everyone who has contact with the person who is going on the diet. One of the first practical ways you could start is by ensuring that everyone is given the opportunity to read this book. Everyone means everyone: grandparents, cousins, uncles and aunts. At school not just the teaching staff, but office, cleaning, maintenance and – especially – dinnertime staff; this really does have to be a team effort.

If you are a teacher with a child in your care who falls into this category then let the parents or carers know that you have this book. It'll go a long way to helping develop a good working relationship in the ultimate interest of the child or children concerned.

Once you're confident that everyone understands the basics then you need to ensure that it's always on everyone's mind and there are some simple measures you can take to help.

At school

- Ask if you can be allocated an area of the staff notice board.

- Head it: Allergy Intolerance and Serious Reactions.

- Pin up this book.

- Prominently display single laminated sheets showing your child's class details with an up-to-date photo.

- Clip his or her individual case history details behind the laminated sheets and include any supportive letters from any medical professionals involved.

- Prominently display a laminated notice in your child's classroom as an aide-memoire. Try to keep it simple; the aim is to act as a constant reminder that your child is on a special diet and only allowed food from a safe source. This will also ensure that other well-meaning parents get the message.

- Make sure there is a protocol in place to ensure that any supply staff read the individual sheets *before* they're let loose in the classroom!

- Update the display regularly.

- Ask for a written process for training new staff at the outset before any inadvertent damage can be done or even better, write it yourself.

- Ensure that the details of the diet, together with the reasoning, are included in the individual education plan.

- Do a classroom 'audit' with the teacher *before* your child starts at the beginning of each term or each new class.

At home

- Gather together email addresses for your friends and family.

- Report regularly on progress.

- Be sure to include failures and successes.

- Send pictures and even copies of behaviour charts.

- If you have a 'pre-diet' or 'mid-reaction' video, offer to let family members watch it.

- Make sure you provide a fully detailed and up-to-date list of the allowed and disallowed foods and non-foods.

- Don't take anything for granted. If in doubt, ask!

- Be constantly on your guard and be a diet detective. Remember, if a child is 'hooked' on something then there is a likelihood that it contains a substance that is causing a problem.

- If a child is still self-limiting his or her diet then there is still a problem in the diet which needs to be identified.

- If a child, despite rigid adherence to dietary and environmental control, is still exhibiting adverse behaviour with aggressive outbursts then bowel problems may be indicated.

- If the week evenings and nights are disruptive but after the weekend everything has settled down then there is a problem at school.

- If there's an infringement, even if you just think there has been, *own up*! Whether you're the parent, carer, teacher, grandma, whoever, discuss it with the team and make sure it's documented. If you don't, and the child has a frightening and painful reaction, it will cause a great deal of angst and everyone will be confused by the sudden adverse reaction, apparently out of the blue. It also risks breaking the bonds of trust which you need to maintain in order to get the best possible outcome for the child.

- Don't panic!

7

Essentials for Teachers and Therapists

Lesson planning

- When planning lessons that include foodstuffs, be aware of the potential risks and identify alternative safe ingredients where possible, such as pasta shape pictures using gluten-free pasta instead of wheat-based pasta or a safe specific carbohydrate diet (SCD) alternative activity.

- Share the plan with the child's parents or guardian well in advance in order to identify alternate strategies and potential hazards. Remember, if you're going to ask the parents to provide an alternative, they are going to need time to go out to buy it, which isn't always that easy with a special needs child.

- If you intend to use food as a reward ensure that it is safe for the diet.

The classroom environment

- Standard glues, paints, felt-tip pens, bubbles and play dough can cause mayhem and the sensitive child may eat them or chew them. Even if they don't put these things in their mouths they will inhale the vapours and absorb the proteins and chemicals through their skin.

- Avoid cross-contamination between anything used or eaten by the other children and the affected child's foods or work materials.

- Make an alternative glue using an acceptable flour or egg white mix. (You can make this into an activity with the child.)

- Make alternative play dough or ask the parents to provide it and keep the child away from proprietary Play-Doh® being used by the others. Better still, let everyone use a gluten-free version (for recipes, see Marilyn Le Breton's *The AiA Gluten and Dairy Free Cookbook*).

- Bubbles and washing up liquid often contain gluten and/or casein, even the eco-friendly versions. Bubbles for blowing can be made up; for relevant information see the cookbook mentioned above, and parents or guardians will advise on suitable washing up liquid.

- Explain to the whole class why the child has to take special precautions and continually monitor for signs of bullying by the other children.

- Ensure 'sitting' mats are made from natural fibres which haven't been coated with anything.

- Keep any animal food well out of the way and find a safe alternative that the child can use to feed the animals. Many small animal foods contain wheat or other unsuitable ingredients.

- The floor polish routinely used in schools is noxious to the children. Try to avoid scheduling lessons for the autistic child in an area newly polished or after it has been shut up for the holiday, weekend and so forth.

- Discourage anyone coming into close contact with the child from using perfume.

The playground

- Ensure all playground duty teachers and parents are fully appraised of the situation and trained accordingly.

- Monitor for bullying and malicious behaviour in the playground in particular.

The dining room

- Instigate a policy of 'no food swaps' throughout the school.

- Instigate a policy of all children washing their hands before and after eating and coming into contact with foodstuffs.

- Make sure the dinner ladies all know about the dangers.

- Make sure the dinner ladies are sensitive to the reasons for the special diet and don't make the child feel more 'different' than he or she already does. A thoughtless word can make lunchtimes a battleground.

- Make sure the child eats at the same table every day after ensuring that both table and chair are wiped down thoroughly before he or she sits down to eat.

- If possible group children who eat the same foods together, otherwise ensure that the other children understand that their food would make the child ill.

Personal hygiene

- Standard soaps contain a host of unsuitable ingredients, ranging from milk and wheat-based additives to colourings and scents. Provide a suitable handwash that should be used at all times.

- Coloured toilet papers may cause immediate irritation which the autistic child may not be able to enunciate.

- If tooth cleaning is included in the school routine then use a suitable toothpaste. Many autistic children eat the toothpaste to get a hit on the ingredients. There are a few, but not many, suitable alternatives.

- Many autistic children suffer from bowel problems, ranging from severe constipation to chronic diarrhoea. Exposure to a food or non-food that they react to can exacerbate the situation.

- Many autistic children have problems with urinary and/or bowel continence when exposed to an offending food or non-food.

Special occasions

- Plan *well ahead* in conjunction with the child's parents or carers. Agree at the beginning of the year what sort of time would be reasonable for the family to organize an alternative.

- Discourage the other parents from sending sweets to school on their child's birthday. A policy disallowing it is best. If you have 40 children in your class and they all bring sweets for the class it's a constant stream of sweets and cakes. If you must tolerate it make sure you have a supply of suitable alternatives for the autistic child so he or she doesn't feel horribly left out.

Risk analysis for all off-site activities

- Off-site activities always present potential risks for the autistic child or adult and full risk analysis for any given trip out should be undertaken. In particular, the needs of the autistic child with dietary or environmental difficulties should be considered well before the trip takes place and not as an afterthought 24 hours before departing!

- Extra attention is needed because of the risk of unforeseen situations – extra supplies of safe rations may need to be included.

- If the trip is to somewhere with children and adults unknown to the class, then extra precautions should be taken to ensure that the child isn't offered sweets or other unsafe foods by anyone. Some autistic children have learned which foods make them ill and are wary or will refuse to accept foods from anyone else but it's safer to assume that they don't know the difference unless you are absolutely certain that they do.

- If the trip includes visiting a shop then thought needs to be given to what is an appropriate purchase for the child to make.

- A copy of the child's individual health plan, medical authorization and emergency procedures should be taken with the group leader, together with an emergency medication kit, including EpiPen® and antihistamine if appropriate, plus antiseptics and plasters all as agreed with the parents or guardian.

- Assign someone to be in charge of the emergency kit to avoid it being left on the bus.

- Do not allow any eating or drinking on the bus.

Emergency training

If the child suffers from classical IgE-mediated allergy, and autistic children and adults *can* suffer from this alongside their other bio-medical problems, then further precautions are essential.

This is what most doctors and lay people recognize as allergy; when the body reacts to an allergen, even the tiniest amount of a substance to which it has become sensitized, by mounting a sudden release of histamine and other chemicals which act on blood vessels causing swelling in the mouth and anywhere on the skin. There is a fall in blood pressure and, in asthma sufferers, the effect is mainly on the lungs. This reaction is known as 'anaphylaxis' and may be fatal if swift action is not taken to medicate with intramuscular adrenaline (epinephrine).

Symptoms are many and even if the ASD child or adult has not been diagnosed with severe allergy, attention should always be paid to the following signs:

- nettle rash (hives) anywhere on the body
- general flushing of the skin
- swelling of throat and mouth
- difficulty in swallowing or speaking
- changes in heart rate
- severe asthma
- abdominal pain, nausea and vomiting
- sudden feeling of weakness (drop in blood pressure)
- collapse and unconsciousness
- steady deterioration.

Remember that many of these symptoms will be difficult to articulate and they can worsen over time so any indication of same should be noted and brought to the attention of a doctor who will assess and refer the case to an allergy specialist if appropriate.

Regular training sessions should take place. These should cover the recognition of symptoms of an allergic reaction as well as the practical administration of medication and injections.

An emergency protocol should be devised in conjunction with the whole team, teachers, drivers, parents or guardians and so on.

An example of a basic school healthcare plan appears in the Resources.

Government guidance on medical needs in schools may be found on the following website: www.teachernet.gov.uk/wholeschool/healthandsafety/medical, while the anaphylaxis campaign sells a range of teaching aids at www.anaphylaxis.org.uk.

Cautionary Tales

There has been a great deal of interest in dietary intervention in the press over the past few years and a host of people have become overnight experts on the subject.

Food manufacturers have been quick to catch on to a lucrative new market and have jumped in at the deep end, often with the unfortunate result that they have produced an array of foods totally unsuitable for the ASD individual because:

- guidelines governing what can legally be called gluten-free food still allow for the inclusion of tiny amounts of gluten

- not everything included in a food has to be declared on the label; there may be any number of ingredients to which the individual reacts, including casein

- cross-contamination in the manufacturing process may allow ingredients through which cause adverse reactions

- derivatives of the offending proteins, for example dextrose, which is widely used in the food industry, made from wheat, can cause severe reactions too.

There really are very few 'safe' processed foods available in the supermarkets, so if a child or adult is on 'diet' but eating a host of packet foods then it's time to start delving deeper.

Not following the intervention properly is a waste of time, effort and money on everyone's part.

Whilst many people have heard of the gluten-free/casein-free (GF/CF) diet in autism spectrum disorder (ASD) they often haven't heard about the sulphation aspect and have no idea about the effect of many of the common additives. Often, people have tried and failed simply owing to a lack of information about what can affect their child and what is going on in the food chain.

People often don't realize that common medicines contain a great number of additives in addition to the pharmacological agents, whilst synthetic sugars, colourings and flavourings are dynamite to the sensitive child or adult.

Shampoos and bath products often contain off-limit ingredients such as casein.

Paints and other play and educational items often contain off-limit ingredients.

9

A Case Study

The following is a short case study of a little boy who started on dietary interventions at the age of five. Although it is impossible to predict the degree of success the intervention can achieve for any individual, this example gives a clear picture of the improvements seen and the beneficial effect not only for the child but for his family, teachers and wider circle.

This little one had already suffered multiple problems in his short life. These comprised, among others and in the order in which he had manifested them, severe colic, sleeplessness and erratic sleep, diarrhoea, asthma, hyperactivity, multiple allergy, complex partial seizures, violent mood swings, food refusal, hypoglycaemia and severe aggression. At the age of three he was diagnosed as autistic with a pragmatic communication disorder on the autistic continuum. The parents said they felt as if they were 'part of a nightmare from which there would be no waking'.

When the child was four and a half his mother, an intelligent and capable lady, was at breaking point and reluctantly approached the consultant requesting a prescription for Ritalin. The consultant agreed, but whilst it provided the family with desperately needed rest, the result was that the boy became so focused that he withdrew further into his own world.

When his mother learned about dietary intervention as a possible tool to help her son, she investigated the rationale and science. Following the recommended steps and working with her doctor and dietician, 12 months later her son was a different child. In a letter his mother wrote:

> It has been very moving to watch the transformation of our child from a frightened, disturbed and crazed bundle of chaos into a sweet, loving (and sometimes mischievous!) little boy. You have, in all honesty, given us our lost child back and there are no words to sufficiently express our gratitude. Our joy is great indeed.

These interventions enabled this young man to start on the road to fulfilling his potential and gaining the most from his educational experiences. The following chart (Figure 9.1) documents the outstanding changes that took place within 12 months of implementation.

Table 9.1 One child's progress after intervention

Start of intervention	*From 4 months to 12 months on diet*
Hyperactive (put on Ritalin, parents could not cope)	Ritalin no longer needed. Now spending 30 minutes or more on what he had previously spent 30 seconds on.
On epilepsy medication for mostly controlled but suspected complex partial seizures plus sedation.	Epilepsy medication no longer needed for seizures or sedation. No sign of epilepsy.
Reactions and behaviours only 10 per cent relevant to situations. In fantasy world and hard to contact.	Very much in our world all the time. Answering questions immediately and picking up on adult conversation not even directed at him. Asking Why? Where? How? What if? questions often.
Compulsive aggression. Could not share. Mood swings. Destructive.	Not aggressive, Starting to share toys, etc. Calm.
Poor sleep. Waking at night.	Sleep much better. Normally goes through night.
Toileting very poor.	Toileting far more reliable.
Asthma often going out of control. Predsol needed every two or three months when we could not stop an ongoing cough.	Asthma under much better control. Predsol not needed since this diet started.
Bowel disturbance. Floating stools. Sometimes constipation, sometimes diarrhoea.	Bowel disturbance not as evident.
Compulsive touching – everyone, everything.	No evidence of compulsive touching.
Abnormal movements.	Reduction in quantity and type of abnormal movements.
Heavy black rings under eyes. Pale.	Eyes and face have very healthy appearance.
Compulsive train talks, and some stereotypical behaviour.	Much broader interests and large decrease in level of stereotypical behaviour.

Start of intervention	*From 4 months to 12 months on diet*
Eating very, very poor. Many times showing signs of hypoglycaemia and no appetite.	Dramatic improvement in appetite and eating three good-sized meals a day.
Extremely difficult to move on from task to task.	Much more willing to move from task to task.
No real empathy. Did not appreciate thoughts and opinions of others.	Asking people for their thoughts and feelings.
No awareness of time and the process of the day.	Much more aware of time and asking questions such as 'Is it time for school now?' and 'Is it the weekend?'
Did not seem to have short-term memory – unconnected thoughts also.	Thoughts less disjointed. Development of short-term memory has started.
Poor long-term memory.	Capacity of long-term memory much greater.
Practically no independent play.	Development of large amounts of independent play. Up to 30 minutes and beyond.
No sense of danger. Had to be on reins whenever out of the house. All trips very difficult. Own agenda.	No problems outside. Walking well alongside adult. Trips out fine, enjoys them. Plays on bike in street with friends. Respects and keeps rules.

10

What You Need
to Know About Ingredients

Dietary gluten and casein sources

Acid whey

All types of cheese (hard and soft)

Acidophilus milk

Artificial butter flavour

Baking soda (some are GF/CF, verify)

Barley malt

Bouillon cubes or powder

Bread

Bulgar wheat

Butter fat

Buttermilk canned milk

Buttermilk solids

Barley (Horedeum vulgare)

Bavarian cream flavouring

Beer bleached all-purpose flour

Bran

Brown sugar flavouring (may contain milk protein)

Butter

Butter flavoured oil

Buttermilk butter solids

Caramel colour

Casein and caseinates
  ammonium caseinate
  calcium caseinate
  magnesium caseinate
  potassium caseinate
  sodium caseinate

Coffee creamer substitute

Cottage cheese

Cream

Cream yoghurt

Cultured milk

Cured whey

Caramel flavouring

Cheese (all types)

Cheese flavour

Cheese food

Chorizo (read label)

Coconut cream flavouring (may contain milk protein)

Condensed milk

Couscous cream

Cream cheese

Croutons

Curds

Custard

Delactosed whey
Dextrin (see page 65)
Dry milk solids
Durum
Durum wheat

Demineralized whey
Dried milk
Dry milks and dry milk ingredients
Durum flour

Edible starch

Evaporated milk

Farina
Filler
Flour (The following may not list every
    unacceptable flour.)
    all-purpose flour
    barley flour
    bread flour
    brown flour
    cake flour
    durum flour
    enriched flour
    Graham flour
    gluten flour
    granary flour
    high gluten flour

Fat-free milk
Flavourings

high protein flour
oat flour
pastry flour
rye flour
semolina flour
seitan flour
spelt
sprouted flour
wheat flour
white flour
wholemeal flour
wholewheat flour

Ice-cream

Ice milk

Kamut

Lactalbumin phosphate
Lactate/lactic acid
Lactose
Low-fat milk

Lactalbumin
Lactoglobulin
Lactulose

Malt
Malt flavouring
Malt vinegar
Margarines (some are dairy-free; read
    labels)
Milk powder
Milk protein hydrolysate
Milk solid pastes
Miso (see page 66)
Modified food starch (verify, may be
    corn or wheat source)
Mustard powder natural colour (verify,
    may be wheat source)

Malt extract
Malt syrup
Malted milk
Milk cheese lactose
Milk fat
Milk protein
Milk solid
Milk solids
Modified starch (verify, may be corn or
    wheat source)
Mononoccum

Natural chocolate flavouring
Non-dairy creamer
Non-fat milk

Natural flavouring (check as may be
    wheat source)
Non-fat milk solids

Oats

Pasta (wheat)
Potassium caseinate
Powdered whey
Pre-packaged broth and gravy

Pearl barley (Job's tears)
Powdered milk
Pre-gelatinized starch (as above)
Pudding rennet casein

Reduced-fat milk
Rice syrup (unless specified gluten-free
    it contains barley enzymes)

Rice malt (contains barley or Koji)
Rye
Rye semolina

Sauce mixes (read labels carefully,
    often contain wheat)
Shoyhu
Skimmed milk powder
Soba noodles
Sodium lactylate (may or may not
    contain casein)
Sour cream solids
Soy sauce (check as may be wheat
    source)
Spelt triticum
Spices (often mixed with wheat flour)
Starch (check as may be wheat source)
Strong flour
Sulphites
Sweet dairy whey
    Two per cent milk

Semolina
Sherbert
Skimmed milk
Small spelt
Sodium lactylate (may or may not
    contain casein)
Sour cream
Imitation solid cream
Spelt
Spices and herbs (buy only those
    specified free of wheat fillers)
Stock cubes (many contain gluten, most
    MSG)
Surimi (verify, may be wheat source)
Sweetened milk
    One per cent milk

Tritical
Triticoseacale
Triticum hard

Teriyaki sauce
Tritical X
Triticum
Triticum vegetable protein

Vegetable gum (check as may be wheat
    source)
Vital gluten

Vegetable starch (check as may be
    wheat source)
Vitamins (check, some contain gluten)

Wheat
Wheat, durum
Wheat gluten

Wheat bran
Wheat germ
Wheat nuts

Wheat oats	Wheat pasta
Wheat starch	Wheat (triticum aestivum)
Whey	Whey concentrate
Whey hydrolysate	Whey powder
Whey protein	Whey protein hydrolysate
Whey sodium caseinate	Whey solids
Whipped cream	White grain
Whole milk	Wholewheat berries
Wholewheat flour	
Yoghurt	Yoghurt powder milk

The above list is to be used as a guideline. Some ingredients may be corn- *or* wheat-derived so you still need to check with the manufacturer. Manufacturers are known to change ingredients listed on labels without warning and they may change the plant derivation of the product according to market prices.

Nitrates/nitrites

There is concern about nitrates or nitrites added to meat. These are preservatives that are added to meats like lunchmeats, bacon, ham, sausage and so on. In particular, they help prevent the growth of botulism bacteria. They also help keep the meat red, instead of grey, which it would soon become without nitrites. Sodium nitrate is additive number E250. Nitrates can easily be converted to nitrites by bacteria in the stomach. They have been shown in an animal study to cause distractibility, and they can also cause headaches. Some parents report their children become hyperactive after eating foods which contain these additives. The decision to eliminate these from your child's diet is a personal one based on how your child reacts after eating foods which contain nitrates/nitrites.

Luncheon meats, sausage and frankfurters: check the labels on luncheon meat, hot dogs and sausages as they may also contain milk protein. Several of the luncheon meats, sausages and frankfurters may contain a grain as an excipient or as a part of a gluten stabilizer.

Additional additive information

- *Calcium disodium.* This additive does *not* contain gluten or casein, but many believe testing is overdue for this additive and it may be harmful.

- *Caramel colour* (may indicate the presence of milk protein). The problem with caramel colour is it may or may not contain gluten depending on how it is manufactured. Note: Dextrose (corn sugar), invert sugar, lactose (milk sugar), malt syrup (usually from barley malt), Molasses (from cane), starch hydrolysate and fractions thereof (can include wheat), sucrose (cane or beet).

- *Cereals.* Most packet breakfast cereals contain malt flavouring, or some other non-gluten-free ingredient.

- *Dextrin* is an incompletely hydrolysed starch. It is prepared by dry-heating corn, waxy maize, waxy milo, potato, arrowroot, *wheat*, rice, tapioca, or sago starches, or by dry-heating the starches after: (1) Treatment with safe and suitable alkalis, acids, or pH-control agents and (2) drying the acid- or alkali-treated starch.

Therefore, unless you know the source, you must avoid dextrin.

- *Miso soybean paste* fermented with barley, rice or other grain. Mono- and di-glycerides can contain a wheat carrier in the USA. While they are derivatives of fats, carbohydrate chains may be used as a binding substance in their preparation, which are usually corn or wheat, so this needs to be checked out with the manufacturer.

- *Rice and soy beverages.* Some production processes ferment rice and soy beverages in barley malt enzymes.

- *Shoyhu.* Soy sauce may utilize a gluten-containing grain or byproduct in the manufacturing process.

- *Sulphites.* Do not contain gluten or casein, but certain individuals may be sensitive to sulphites. They have been known to cause breathing problems, violent headaches, dizziness, hives and abdominal pain in certain sensitive individuals.

- *Wheat starch.* Most coeliac organizations in the USA and Canada do not believe that wheat starch is safe for coeliacs. In Europe, however, Codex Alimentarius-quality wheat starch is considered acceptable in the coeliac diet by most doctors and coeliac organizations. This is a higher quality of wheat starch than is generally available in the USA or Canada, but care must be taken when using coeliac food lists as the vast majority of ASD children and adults are intolerant of *all* wheat starch.

Always watch out for cross-contamination, for example wheat breadcrumbs in butter, jams, toasters, kitchen surfaces and so on. Look out for banned ingredients in lotions, creams and cosmetics, stamps, envelopes or other gummed labels, toothpaste and mouthwash and don't forget that even if something is labelled as containing 'natural flavouring' *avoid it*. Remember, if in doubt, contact the manufacturer.

Monosodium glutamate (MSG E621)

Monosodium glutamate does not contain gluten or casein but children react adversely. Avoid the following:

- Autolysed yeast (7–24 per cent)
- Barley malt (not GF/CF)
- Calcium caseinate (not GF/CF)
- E621 (78.2 per cent)
- E622 (78.2 per cent)
- Gelatine (11–12 per cent)
- Glutamate (95 per cent)
- Glutamic acid (95 per cent)
- Glutamic acid levels identified as DGA
- Hydrolyzed protein (20–40 per cent)
- Malt extract (not GF/CF)
- MSG/monosodium glutamate (78.2 per cent)
- MPG/monopotassium glutamate (78.2 per cent)

- Sodium caseinate (not GF/CF)
- Soya protein concentrate (exact figure not known, expected to be as hydrolysed protein)
- Soya protein isolate (exact figure not known, expected to be as above)
- Textured/texturized protein (exact figure not known, expected to be as above)
- Yeast extract (7–24 per cent)
- Yeast food* (7–24 per cent)
- Yeast nutrient* (7–24 per cent)

Always check the labels of the foods you prepare as manufacturers are known to change ingredients without warning!

Aspartame

Aspartame does *not* contain gluten or casein but it is recommended that all foods containing this additive should be avoided. This is *not* a healthy additive for anyone, regardless of GF/CF status. This means that all sugar-free foods should be checked very carefully.

Particular nasties

- Fructose
- Mannitol
- Saltpetre
- Sodium benzoate
- Sodium nitrate

- Sodium nitrite
- Sorbitol
- Vanilla – highly phenolic
- Vanillan – highly phenolic

Medicines

This is usually a problem of additional colouring, flavouring or artificial sugars, but there may also be gluten in the mix. Check with the manufacturers and ask to speak to the production director if there is a problem. It is often possible to do a production run without extra additives. There is a risk of cross-contamination but this must be weighed up against the need for the medicine.

Check all the ingredients on every label every time!

Salicylates

This is a list of commonly used foods which are high or very high in salicylates. It isn't exhaustive but provides a good basic guide.

All dried fruits	Almond
Aniseed	Apricot
Avocado	
Basil	Black pepper
Blackberry	Blackcurrant
Blueberry	Boysenberry
Canned green olives	Capsicum
Cayenne	Celery powder
Champignon	Cherries

Chewing gum	Chicory
Chilli flakes	Chilli peppers
Chilli powder	Cider vinegar
Coconut oil	Commercial gravies and sauces
Courgette	Cranberry
Cumin	Currant
Curry	
Date	Dill
Endive	
Fenugreek	Fish, meat, and tomato pastes
Garam masala	Gherkins
Ginger	Grape
Guava	
Honey	Honey flavours
Hot pepper	
Jam (except pear, preferably homemade)	Jam/jelly (all commercial varieties – you can make your own from acceptable ingredients)
Liquorices	Loganberry
Mace	Marmite®
Mint	Mint-flavoured sweets
Mustard	
Nutmeg	
Olive oil	Orange
Oregano	

Paprika	Peanuts with skins on
Peppermint	Peppermints
Peppers	Pineapple
Plum	Prune
Radish	Raisin
Raspberry	Redcurrant
Rock melon	Rosemary
Sage	Strawberry
Sultana	
Tabasco	Tangerine
Tarragon	Thyme
Tomato	Tomato products
Turmeric	
Water chestnut	White pepper
White vinegar	Wine vinegar
Worcester sauce	

Marmite® and other yeast extracts

Youngberry

11

The Last Word

From the Autism Medical forum

hello. i am off school today becos my tummy is still not good cos now i am having no shuger for a littel bit. i have been on a speshal diet for a long time now but since doing a proper one i am not shouted at so much and i can read and rite. i read a full book on my own last nite. i am not very good at maths yet but i cud be one day. my ears don't buzz now and i can hear much better. i can't have milk, eggs which make me get spots all over nad i can't breeth, and gluten and loads of things but mum can still cook really good food and now i am not pooing all my mussles out so i can do press ups. my teachers are very happy that i can sit down but it is still hard to understnd sometimes. i can listen at tiekwondo really good now. mum think sthe best thing is that i hold her hand and wark insted of jumping all the time but i think i look silly. i hope you all make your children have speshal diets too because then they will be happier. thank you from joe jackson who is 8 oon the 29th of march

I can't add a lot to what Joe has just said only to say that he is ADHD [attention deficit hyperactivity disorder]

and possibly has Asperger syndrome (AS). He has been GF/CF [gluten-free/caseine-free] for many years... however, so many things had traces of gluten in them that he was in a constant state of withdrawal and so has spent his life craving, and stealing all off-limits foods. His brother is 12 and has Asperger's and his little brother is four and quite severely autistic. He can now talk since going GF/CF.

They have all been transformed by the diet and if anyone thinks that they cannot begin to embark on the diet then if I can do it, so can you! There is all the help you need at your finger tips so go for it – there is nothing to lose and so much to gain! (Jacqui Jackson)

12

Resources

Checklist of common classic symptoms

This quick and easy checklist will give you an immediate indication of whether or not diet or bowel problems or both, are a feature to investigate further.

- [ ] Breaking wind frequently
- [ ] Red face and/or ears
- [ ] Pale skin/pasty face
- [ ] Giggling/screaming for no apparent reason
- [ ] Eats non-foods, e.g. earth, sand, paper, soap
- [ ] Excessive sweating, especially at night
- [ ] Craving/dislike for certain foods
- [ ] Limits foods
- [ ] Inability to control body temperature
- [ ] Dark shadows or rings under the eyes
- [ ] Family members with allergy (asthma, eczema, hay fever, migraine, etc.)
- [ ] Family members with pernicious anaemia

- ☐ Family members with gut disorders (Crohn's disease, ulcerative colitis, coeliac disease, etc.)
- ☐ Adopts strange positions
- ☐ Hyperactive before a bowel movement
- ☐ Lack of bladder control
- ☐ Lack of bowel control
- ☐ Bloating
- ☐ Swollen tummy
- ☐ Diarrhoea
- ☐ Constipation
- ☐ Always hungry
- ☐ Never hungry
- ☐ Oblivious to pain
- ☐ Unidentified rashes that come and go
- ☐ Coarse dry hair

Explanation of charts
School healthcare plan

The school healthcare plan is deliberately large so that important information may be spotted immediately in an emergency. This plan is specifically aimed at the child or adult with food and environmental intolerances and allergies, but can be adapted for other uses. In the UK the school is not legally obliged to administer medications, though most will and are indemnified by their insurance. If staff want to volunteer to be trained in administering medication, and the most likely scenario here is the use of an EpiPen® to administer life-saving adrenaline, then no one can stop them. The best thing you can do is to ensure that a copy of this plan is attached to the information on your section of the school notice board and that everyone knows that it's there.

Food diary

The food diary is filled in to provide an accurate daily record of food, drink and vitamin or mineral intake. Completion of a food diary is essential prior to dietary intervention and at appropriate intervals to keep a check on the dietary balance. You will need to use one per day for a minimum of three days, though five days is better and the dietician will analyse the total intake highlighting any deficits or imbalances against government recommended daily allowances (RDAs). Whilst there are cases for increased intake of certain vitamins and minerals, the point of the food diary is to obtain a baseline from which to work.

Food/behaviour diary

This chart is the main workhorse of dietary intervention and will show up patterns of behaviour which you may not previously have spotted. Ensure that one accompanies your child wherever he or she goes and show staff how to fill it in. It doesn't have to be laborious as long as everything of relevance is noted so that you can understand it yourself when you look back on it. You might want to invent shorthand for types of behaviour to make it quicker and easier to fill in.

School health care plan

Child's details

Full name:

Class:

Home Address:

Date of Birth:

NHS Number:

Hospital Number:

EMERGENCY CONTACT DETAILS

Name of Parent /Guardian:

☎ Home Telephone:

☎ Work Telephone:

📱 Mobile Number:

Name of 2nd Contact:

Relationship to Child:

☎ Home Telephone:

☎ Work Telephone:

📱 Mobile Number:

GP Details:

Name of GP:

☎ Surgery Telephone:

Medication: Name(s) with expiry details

Name	Where Stored	Expiry Date

Training

Staff Volunteer Names	Department/Contact Details	Date Last Formal Training

Nature of Allergy/Intolerance

Consent and Agreement of Parent/Carer

I agree to the staff taking responsibility for administering the above medication in the event of a reaction taking place.

Name of Parent/Carer:

Signature:

Food Diary

Name: _____ Date: _____ Day Number: _____ Completed by: _____

Time	Food/Drink	Brand	Ingredients	Amount	Leftover	Bowels/Urine	Observation

Additional Notes:

Food/ Behaviour Diary

Name: _____ Date: _____ Day Number: _____ Completed by: _____

Time	Food/ Drink	Vits/ Minerals	Medicine	Behaviour	Appearance	Bowels/ Urine	Sleep Pattern

Additional notes:

Suggested reading

There are now hundreds of books and websites on the subject of diet, autism and ADHD, but you are reading this one because you haven't the time to plough your way through all of them so this is a *short* list of essentials.

- What it says on the title and still the best compilation cookbook that includes recipes for non-food items like gluten-free play dough:

The AiA Gluten and Dairy Free Cookbook
Compiled by: Marilyn Le Breton
Publisher: Jessica Kingsley Publishers
ISBN 978 1 84310 067 6

- If you want to know more about the specific carbohydrate diet then Elaine Gottschall's book is a must. Recently deceased, her career championing the work of Dr Haas has been, and will continue to be, of inestimable value:

Breaking the Vicious Cycle: Intestinal Health Through Diet
Author: Elaine G. Gottschall
Publisher: Kirkton PR Ltd; Revised edition (Aug 1994)
ISBN 978 0 96927 681 4

- If the low oxalate approach is necessary then the following cook book includes oxalate values:

The Low Oxalate Cookbook, Book 2
Authors: The VP Foundation
Publisher: The VP Foundation
ISBN 978 0 96562 231 8

Bibliography

The following is a small selection, a taster if you like, of the range of medical papers written about diet in autism and other disorders on the same spectrum. There are many, many more, so don't let anyone brush you aside with the unfounded comment that there is no medical evidence surrounding dietary intervention in autism!

(2004) 'Mechanisms of non-IgE mediated adverse reaction to common dietary proteins (DPs) in children with autism spectrum disorders (ASD).' Conference.

Alberti, A., Pirrone, P., Elia, M., Waring, R.H. and Romano, C. (1999) 'Sulphation deficit in "low-functioning" autistic children: a pilot study.' *Biological Psychiatry 46*, 420–424.

Alpers, D.H. (1986) 'Uptake and fate of absorbed amino acids and peptides in the mammalian intestine.' *Federation Proceedings 45*, 2261–2267.

Ashwood, P., Anthony, A., Torrente, F. and Wakefield, A.J. (2004) 'Spontaneous mucosal lymphocyte cytokine profiles in children with autism and gastrointestinal symptoms: mucosal immune activation and reduced counter regulatory interleukin-10.' *Journal of Clinical Immunology 24*, 664–673.

Ashkenazi, A., Krasilowsky, D., Levin, S., Idar, D. *et al.* (1979) 'Immunologic reaction of psychotic patients to fractions of gluten.' *American Journal of Psychiatry 136*, 1306–1309.

Barthelemy, C., Bruneau, N., Adrien, J., Roux, S. and Lelord, G. (1990) 'Clinical, biological and therapeutic applications of the functional analysis of autistic disorders.' *Brain Dysfunction 3*, 271–284.

Bidet, B., Leboyer, M., Descours, B., Bouvard, M.P. and Benveniste, J. (1993) 'Allergic sensitization in infantile autism.' *Journal of Autism and Developmental Disorders 23*, 419–420.

Bouvard, M.P., Leboyer, M., Launay, J.M., Recasens, C. *et al.* (1992) 'The opioid excess hypothesis of autism: a double-blind study of naltrexon. Proceedings of the International Symposium on Neurobiology of Infantile Autism, 1990, Neurobiology of Infantile Autism.' *Exerpta Medica.*

Bouvard, M.P., Leboyer, M., Launay, J.M., Recasens, C. *et al.* (1995) 'Low-dose naltrexone effects on plasma chemistries and clinical symptoms in autism: a double-blind, placebo-controlled study.' *Psychiatry Research 58*, 191–201.

Brantl, V. and Teschemacher, H. (1979) 'A material with opioid activity in bovine milk and milk products.' *Archives of Pharmacology 306*, 301–304.

Bull, G., Shattock, P., Whiteley, P., Anderson, R. *et al.* (2003) 'Indoly-3-acryloylglycine (IAG) is a putative diagnostic urinary marker for autism spectrum disorders.' *Medical Science Monitor 9*, CR422–425.

Cade, R., Wayemaker, H., Privelten, R.M., Fregly, M.S. *et al.* (1990) 'The effects of dialysis and diet in schizophrenia.' *Psychiatry: A World Perspective 3*, 494–500.

Cade, J.R. *et al.* (1999) 'Autism and schizophrenia linked to malfunctioning enzyme for milk protein digestion.' *Autism*

Cade, J.R., Privette, R.M., Fregly, M., Rowland, N. *et al.* (1999) 'Autism and schizophrenia: Intestinal disorders.' *Nutritional Neuroscience 2*, 57–72.

Carroccio, A., Montalto, G., Custro, N., Notarbartolo, A. *et al.* (2000) 'Evidence of very delayed clinical reactions to cow's milk in cow's milk-intolerant patients.' *Allergy 55*, 574–579.

Cavataio, F., Carroccio, A. and Iacono, G. (2000) 'Milk-induced reflux in infants less than one year of age.' *Journal of Pediatric Gastroenterology and Nutrition 30 (Suppl.),* S36–44.

Chang, K.J., Su, Y.F., Brent, D.A. and Chang, J.K. (1985) 'Isolation of a specific mu-opiate receptor peptide, morphiceptin, from an enzymatic digest of milk proteins.' *Journal of Biological Chemistry 260*, 9706–9712.

Cooke, W.T. and Smith, W.T. (1966) 'Neurological disorders associated with adult celiac disease.' *Brain 89*, 683–722.

Cornish, E. (2002) 'Gluten and casein free diets in autism: a study of the effects on food choice and nutrition.' *Journal of Human Nutrition and Diet 15*, 261–269.

Dohan, F.C. (1966) 'Cereals and schizophrenia: data and hypothesis.' *Acta Psychiatrica Scandinavica 42*, 125–152.

Bibliography

Dohan, F.C. (1966) 'Wheat "consumption" and hospital admissions for schizophrenia during World War II. A preliminary report.' *American Journal of Clinical Nutrition 18*, 7–10.

Dohan, F.C. (1969) 'Is celiac disease a clue to pathogenesis of schizophrenia?' *Mental Hygiene 53*, 525–529.

Dohan, F.C. (1979) 'Schizophrenia and neuroactive peptides from food.' *Lancet 1*, 1031.

Dohan, F.C. (1988) 'Genetic hypothesis of idiopathic schizophrenia: its exorphin connection.' *Schizophrenia Bulletin 14*, 489–494.

Dohan, F.C. and Grasberger, J.C. (1973) 'Relapsed schizophrenics: earlier discharge from the hospital after cereal-free, milk-free diet.' *American Journal of Psychiatry 130*, 685–688.

Dohan, F.C., Harper, E.H., Clark, M.H., Rodrige, R.B. and Zigas, B.. (1984) 'Is schizophrenia rare if grain is rare?' *Biological Psychiatry 19*, 385–399.

Dubynin, V.A., Ivleva, I, A., Malinovskaia, I.V., Kamenskii, A.A. *et al.* (2001) 'Changes in beta-casomorphine-7 effect on behavior of albino rat pups in postnatal development [in Russian].' *Zhurnal Vysshei Nervnoi Deiatelnosti Imeni I.P. Pavlova 51*, 386–389.

Dubynin, V.A., Maklakova, A.S., Nezavibat'ko, V.N., Alfeeva, L.A. *et al.* (1992) 'Effects of systemically-administered beta-casomorphin-7 on nociception in rats [in Russian].' *Biulleten Eksperimentalnoi Biologii I Meditsiny 114*, 284–286.

Ek, J., Stensrud, M. and Reichelt, K.L. (1990) 'Gluten-free diet decreases urinary peptide levels in children with celiac disease.' *Journal of Pediatric Gastroenterology and Nutrition 29*, 282–285.

Fukudome, S.-I. and Yoshikawa, M. (1991) 'Opioid peptides derived from wheat gluten: their isolation and characterization.' *FEBS Letters 296*, 107–111.

Fukudome, S. and Yoshikawa, M. (1992) 'Opioid peptides derived from wheat gluten: their isolation and characterization.' *Federation of European Biochemical Societies (FEBS) Letters 296*, 107–111.

Fukudome, S. and Yoshikawa, M. (1993) 'Gluten exorphin C, a novel opioid peptide derived from wheat gluten.' *FEBS Letters 316*, 17–19.

Fukudome, S. *et al.* (1997) 'Release of opioid peptides, gluten exorphins by the action of pancreatic elastase.' *FEBS Letters 412*, 475–479.

Furlano, R.I., Anthony, A., Day, R., Brown, A. *et al.* (2001) 'Colonic CD8 and gamma delta T-cell infiltration with epithelial damage in children with autism.' *Journal of Pediatrics 138*, 366–372.

Gardner, M.L.G. (1983) 'Evidence for, and implications of, passage of intact peptides across the intestinal mucosa.' *Biochemical Society Transactions 11*, 810–812.

Gardner, M.L.G. (1994) 'Absorption of Intact Proteins and Peptides.' In L.R. Johnson (ed.) *Physiology of the Gastrointestinal Tract,* 3rd ed. New York, NY: Raven Press.

Garvey, J. (2002) 'Diet in autism and associated disorders.' *Journal of Family Health Care 12,* 34–38.

Goodwin, M.S., Cowen, M.A. and Goodwin, T.C. (1971) 'Malabsorption and cerebral dysfunction: a multivariate and comparative study of autistic children.' *Journal of Autism and Child Schizophrenia 1,* 48–62.

Hadjivassiliou, M., Boscolo, S., Davies-Jones, G.A., Grunewald, R.A. *et al.* (2002)'The humoral response in the pathogenesis of gluten ataxia.' *Neurology 58,* 1221–1226.

Hadjivassiliou, M., Gibson, A., Davies-Jones, G.A., Lobo, A.J., Stephenson, T.J. and Milford-Ward, A. (1996) 'Does cryptic gluten sensitivity play a part in neurological illness?' *Lancet 347,* 369–371.

Hadjivassiliou, M., Grunewald, R.A., Lawden, M., Davies-Jones, G.A., Powell, T. and Smith, C.M. (2001) 'Headache and CNS white matter abnormalities associated with gluten sensitivity.' *Neurology 56,* 385–388.

Hadjivassiliou, M., Grunewald, R.A. and Davies-Jones, G.A. (2002) 'Gluten sensitivity as a neurological illness.' *Journal of Neurology, Neurosurgery and Psychiatry 72,* 560–563.

Herrera-Marschitz, M., Terenius, L., Grehn, L. and Ungerstedt, U. (1989) 'Rotational behaviour produced in intranigral injections of bovine and human beta-casomorphins in rats.' *Psychopharmacology 99,* 357–361.

Hole, K., Bergslien, A.A., Jørgensen, H., Bergen, O.-G., Reichelt, K.L. and Trygstad, O.E. (1979) 'A peptide containing fraction from schizophrenia which stimulates opiate receptors and inhibits dopamine uptake.' *Neuroscience 4,* 1139–1147.

Hole, K., Lingjaerde, O., Mørkrid, L., Bøler, J.B. *et al.* (1988) 'Attention deficit disorders: a study of peptide-containing urinary complexes.' *Journal of Developmental and Behavioral Pediatrics 9,* 205–212.

Huebner, F.R., Lieberman, K.W., Rubino, R.P. and Wall, J.S. (1984) 'Demonstration of high opioid-like activity in isolated peptides from wheat gluten hydrolysates.' *Peptides 5,* 1139–1147.

Iacono, G., Cavataio, F., Montalto, G., Florena, A. *et al.* (1998) 'Intolerance of cow's milk and chronic constipation in children.' *New England Journal of Medicine 339,* 1100–1104.

Jyonouchi, H., Geng, L., Ruby, A. and Zimmerman-Bier, B. (2005) 'Dysregulated innate immune responses in young children with autism spectrum disorders: their relationship to gastrointestinal symptoms and dietary intervention.' *Neuropsychobiology 51,* 77–85.

Jyonouchi, H., Geng, L., Ruby, A., Reddy, C. and Zimmerman-Bier, B. (2005) 'Evaluation of an association between gastrointestinal symptoms and cytokine production against common dietary proteins in children with autism spectrum disorders.' *Journal of Pediatrics 146*, 605–610.

Jyonouchi, H., Sun, S. and Le, H. (2001) 'Proinflammatory and regulatory cytokine production associated with innate and adaptive immune responses in children with autism spectrum disorders and developmental regression.' *Journal of Neuroimmunology 120*, 170–179.

Kahn, A., Rebuffat, E., Blum, D., Casimir, G. *et al.* (1987) 'Difficulty in initiating and maintaining sleep associated with cow's milk allergy in infants.' *Sleep 10*, 116–121.

Kidd, P.M. (2002) 'Autism, an extreme challenge to integrative medicine. Part 1: the knowledge base.' *Alternative Medicine Review 7*, 292–316.

Kidd, P.M. (2002) 'Autism, an extreme challenge to integrative medicine. Part 2: medical management.' *Alternative Medicine Review 7*, 472–499.

Knivsberg, A.M., Reichelt, K.L. and Nodland, M. (2001) 'Reports on dietary intervention in autistic disorders.' *Nutritional Neuroscience 4*, 25–37.

Knivsberg, A.M., Reichelt, K.L., Hoien, T. and Nodland, M. (2002) 'A randomised, controlled study of dietary intervention in autistic symptoms.' *Nutritional Neuroscience 5*, 251–261.

Knivsberg, A.M., Reichelt, K.L., Nodland, M. and Hoien, T. (1995) 'Autistic syndromes and diet. A four year follow-up study.' *Scandinavian Journal of Education Research 39*, 223–236.

Knivsberg, A.M., Wiig, K., Lind, G., Nodland, M. and Reichelt, K.L. (1990) 'Dietary intervention in autistic syndromes.' *Brain Dysfunction 3*, 315–327.

Kurek, M., Czerwionka-Szaflarska, M. and Doroszewska, G. (1995) 'Pseudoallergic skin reactions to opiate sequences of bovine casein in healthy children.' *Roczniki Adademii Medycznez W Bialymstoku 40*, 480–485.

Kurek, M., Przybilla, B., Hermann, K. and Ring, J. (1992) 'A naturally occurring opioid peptide from cow's milk, beta-casomorphine-7, is a direct histamine releaser in man.' *International Archives in Allergy and Immunology 97*, 115–120.

Leboyer, M., Bouvard, M.P., Lensing, P., Launay, J.M. *et al.* (1990) 'Opioid excess hypothesis of autism.' *Brain Dysfunction 3*, 285–298.

Leboyer, M., Bouvard, M.P., Launay, J.M., Recasens, C. *et al.* (1993) 'Opiate hypothesis in infantile autism? Therapeutic trials with naltrexone [in French].' *Encephale 19*, 95–102.

Lensing, P., Klingler, D., Lampl, C. and Leboyer, M. (1992) 'Naltrexone open trial with a 5-year-old boy. A social rebound reaction.' *Acta Paedopsychiatrica 55*, 169–173.

Lensing, P., Schimke, H., Klimesch, W., Pap, V. *et al.* (1995) 'Clinical case report: opiate antagonist and event-related desynchronization in 2 autistic boys.' *Neuropsychobiology 31*, 16–23.

Lindstrom, L.H., Nyberg, F., Terenius, L., Bauer, K. *et al.* (1984) 'CSF and plasma beta-casomorphin-like opioid peptides in post-partum psychosis.' *American Journal of Psychiatry 141*, 1059–1066.

Longoni, R., Spina, L., Mulas, A., Carboni, E. *et al.* (1991) '(D-Ala2) deltorphin II: D1-dependent stereotypes and stimulation of dopamine release in the nucleus accumbens.' *Journal of Neuroscience 11*, 1565–1576.

Lucarelli, S., Frediani, T., Zingoni, A.M., Ferruzzi, F. *et al.* (1995) 'Food allergy and infantile autism.' *Panminerva Medicine 37*, 137–141.

Loukas, S., Varoucha, D., Zioudrou, C., Streaty, R.A. and Klee, W.A. (1983) 'Opioid activities and structures of alpha-casein-derived exorphins.' *Biochemistry 22*, 4567–4573.

Marchetti, B., Scifo, R., Batticane, N. and Scapagnini, U. (1990) 'Immunological significance of opioid peptide dysfunction in infantile autism.' *Brain Dysfunction 3*, 346–354.

Meisel, H. (1986) 'Chemical characterization and opioid activity of an exorphin isolated from in vivo digests of casein.' *FEBS Letters 196*, 223–227.

Millward, C., Ferriter, M., Calvers, S. and Connell-Jones, G. (2004) 'Gluten- and casein-free diets for autistic spectrum disorder.' *Cochrane Database Systematic Reviews 2*, CD003498.

Morley, J.E. (1982) 'Food peptides. A new class of hormones?' *Journal of the American Medical Association 247*, 2379–2380.

O'Banion, D., Armstrong, B., Cummings, R.A. and Stange, J. (1978) 'Disruptive behavior: a dietary approach.' *Journal of Autism and Child Schizophrenia 8*, 325–337.

Paroli, E. (1988) 'Opioid peptides form food (the exorphins).' *World Review of Nutrition and Dietetics 55*, 58–97.

Pedersen, O.S., Liu, Y. and Reichelt, K.L. (1999) 'Serotonin uptake stimulating peptide found in plasma of normal individuals and in some autistic urines.' *Journal of Peptide Research 53*, 641–646.

Pfeiffer, C.C. (1984) 'Schizophrenia and wheat gluten enteropathy.' *Biological Psychiatry 19*, 279–280.

Ramabadran, K. and Bansinath, M. (1988) 'Opioid peptides from milk as a possible cause of sudden infant death syndrome.' *Medical Hypotheses 27*, 181–187.

Reichelt, K.L., Ekrem, J. and Scott, H. (1990) 'Gluten, milk proteins and autism: dietary interventions effects on behavior and peptide secretion.' *Journal of Applied Nutrition 42*, 1–11.

Reichelt, K.L. and Knivsberg, A.M. (2003) 'Can the pathophysiology of autism be explained by the nature of the discovered urine peptides?' *Nutritional Neuroscience 6*, 19–28.

Reichelt, K.L., Hole, K., Hamberger, A., Saelid, G. *et al.* (1981) 'Biologically active peptide-containing fractions in schizophrenia and childhood autism.' *Advances in Biochemical Psychopharmacology 28*, 627–643.

Reichelt, K.L., Knivsberg, A.M., Lind, G. and Nodland, M. (1991) 'The probable etiology and possible treatment of childhood autism.' *Brain Dysfunction 4*, 308–319.

Reichelt, K.L., Knivsberg, A.M., Nodland, M. and Lind, G. (1994) 'Nature and consequences of hyperpeptiduria and bovine casomorphin found in autistic syndromes.' *Developing Brain Dysfunction 7*, 71–85.

Risebro, B. (1991) 'Gluten-free diet in infantile autism.' *Tidsskrift for den Norske Laegeforening 111*, 1885–1186.

Rix, K.J., Ditchfield, J., Freed, D.L., Goldberg, D.P. and Hillier, V.F. (1985) 'Food antibodies in acute psychoses.' *Psychological Medicine 15*, 347–354.

Saelid, G. Haug, J.O., Heiberg, T. and Reichelt, K.L. (1985) 'Peptide-containing fractions in depression.' *Biological Psychiatry 20*, 245–256.

Sahley, T.L. and Panksepp, J. (1987) 'Brain opioids and autism: an updated analysis of possible linkages.' *Journal of Autism and Developmental Disorders 17*, 201–216.

Scifo, R., Cioni, M., Nicolois, A., Batticane, N. *et al.* (1996) 'Opioid-immune interactions in autism: behavioral and immunological assessment during a double-blind treatment with naltrexone.' *Annali dell' Instituto superiore di sanità 32*, 351–359.

Shattock, P., Kennedy, A., Rowell, F. and Berney, T. (1990) 'Role of neuropeptides in autism and their relationships with classical neurotransmitters.' *Brain Dysfunction 3*, 328–246.

Sun, Z. and Cade, J.R. (1999) 'A peptide found in schizophrenia and autism causes behavioral changes in rats.' *Autism 3*, 85.

Sun, Z., Cade, J.R., Fregly, M.J. and Privette, R.M. (1999) 'Casomorphine induces Fos-like reactivity in discrete brain regions relevant to schizophrenia and autism.' *Autism 3*, 67–84.

Svedberg, J., de Haas, J., Leimenstdl, G., Paul, F. and Teschemacher, H. (1985) 'Demonstration of beta-casomorphin immunoreactive materials in in vitro digests of bovine milk and in small intestine contents after bovine milk ingestion in adult humans.' *Peptides 6*, 825–830.

Takahashi, M., Fukunaga, H., Kaneto, H., Fukudome, S. and Yoshikawa, M. (2000) 'Behavioral and pharmacological studies on gluten exorphin A5, a newly isolated bioactive food protein fragment, in mice.' *Japanese Journal of Pharmacology 84*, 259–265.

Teschemacher, H. and Koch, G. (1991) 'Opioids in the milk.' *Endocrine Regulation 25*, 147–150.

Teschemacher, H. Koch, G. and Brautl, V. (1997) 'Milk protein-derived opioid receptor ligands.' *Biopolymers 43*, 99–117.

Trygstad, O.E., Reichelt, K.L., Foss, I., Edminson, P.D. (1980) 'Patterns of peptides and protein-associated-peptide complexes in psychiatric disorders.' *British Journal of Psychiatry 136*, 59–72.

Vojdani, A., Bazargan, M., Vojdani, E., Samadi, J. *et al.* (2004) 'Heat shock protein and gliadin peptide promote development of peptidase antibodies in children with autism and patients with autoimmune disease.' *Clinical and Diagnostic Laboratory Immunology 11*, 515–524.

Vojdani, A., Campbell, A.W., Anyanwu, E., Kashanian, A., Bock, K. and Vojdani, E. (2002) 'Antibodies to neuron-specific antigens in children with autism: possible cross-reaction with encephalitogenic proteins from milk, Chlamydia pneumoniae and Streptococcus group.' *American Journal of Neuroimmunology 129*, 168–177.

Vojdani, A., O'Bryan, T., Green, J.A., Mccandless, J. *et al.* (2004) 'Immune response to dietary proteins, gliadin and cerebellar peptides in children with autism.' *Nutritional Neuroscience 7*, 151–161.

Vojdani, A., Pangborn, J.B., Vojdani, E. and Cooper, E.L. (2003) 'Infections, toxic chemicals and dietary peptides binding to lymphocyte receptors and tissue enzymes are major instigators of autoimmunity in autism.' *International Journal of Immunopathology and Pharmacology 16*, 189–199.

Wakefield, A.J., Puleston, J.M., Montgomery, S.M., Anthony, A., O'Leary, J.J. and Murch, S.H. (2002) 'Review article: the concept of entero-colonic encephalopathy, autism and opioid receptor ligands.' *Alimentary Pharmacology and Therapeutics 16*, 663–674.

White, J.F. (2003) 'Intestinal pathophysiology in autism.' *Experimental Biological Medicine 228*, 639–649.

Whiteley, P. and Shattock, P. (2002) 'Biochemical aspects in autism spectrum disorders: updating the opioid-excess theory and presenting new opportunities for biomedical intervention.' *Expert Opinion and Therapeutic Targets 6*, 175–183.

Zioudrou, C., Streaty, R.A. and Klee, W.A. (1979) 'Opioid peptides derived from food proteins. The exorphins.' *Journal of Biological Chemistry 254*, 2446–2449.

Index